GW00544507

POEMS

from the

TOGETHER!

POP-UP POETRY CLUB

Edited by

SARAH HUGHES

First published in Great Britain
by Bettany Press, 2014.
8 Kildare Road London E16 4AD.

Text © the authors 2014.

British Library Cataloguing in Publication Data.
A catalogue record for this book is available
from the British Library.

ISBN 978-1-908304-17-9

Contents

Carla Aveleira

Together! Poet Carla Aveleira writes: "I am from Portugal and have been living in the UK since 2004. I wrote the first poem, 'Confusion', to tell about my experience with health services when I had a mental breakdown. At that time I was also studying for a mental health nursing degree."

Confusion

Being on both sides of the system
I feel awkward for seeking help
How can I say I am not coping?
How can I say I can't sleep?
They are coping
They are working
Their lives seem to proceed
I feel that I am being judged
I feel intimidated indeed
I feel misunderstood
They don't seem to notice me
I shout, I complain
But my voice is unheard
Does that surprise you?
Are you not able to see?
I am not a professional
I am a patient and I want to be treated fairly.

Encouragement

We all need words of encouragement
No matter our background
There will always be days
That we need to be picked up from the ground

You are worthy of my friendship
You are a good person indeed
You deserve happiness
You will get everything you need.

Old Friend

You were my sister my friend
The one I trusted the most
You knew all my secrets
And I knew all of yours

We gave equally
We valued what we had
It was sad to let you go
There's a space empty in my heart.

Dawn Barber

Together! Poet Dawn Barber writes: "I am 47 years old. Since I have been writing poetry I have become more confident and stronger in myself. It has made me open up more and I am so glad to be around such lovely people who give me the strength to go on and cope with my depression."

Fear

When the lady runs along the road at night
knowing that someone is coming after her

FEAR SETS IN.

Her heart beats so fast.

She sweats. She shakes. She has to try to find
somewhere to hide.
Will she find that place?

FEAR

Talking to God

God, let your love be upon me,
Please give me more peace of mind.
Take me by the hand and hold onto me tight.
When I cry, please wipe away my tears.
I love you.
Dear God.

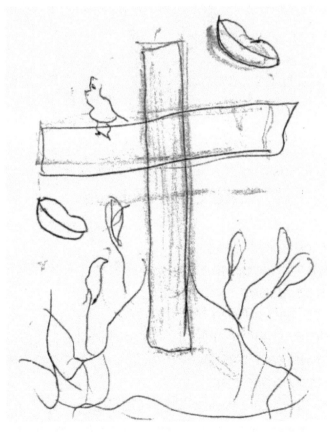

The Cave of Love

They meet in a cave
He kissed her on the hands
She had missed him so much
And he had missed her too
Suddenly they heard a noise and looked up
And they saw the face of God
And they smiled and
knew their love would last FOREVER.

We hate you, Cancer

Cancer—you're a horrible illness
People don't need you in their lives
You're poison! You're cruel. You're a killer.
We all hate you and you turn our lives upside
down and eat us away.
I only hope one day there will be a cure to destroy
you
and eat you away like you do to us.
WE WILL NOT LET YOU WIN.

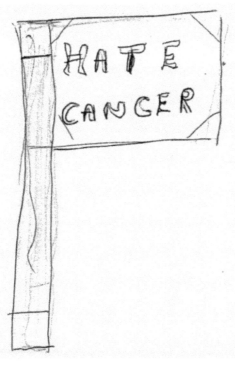

Mary Ann and Stan

They called her MARY ANN.
She was married to a man named STAN,
They went to church every Sunday
and said their prayers at night.
They would sit near the fire
on those cold winter nights.
They were such a nice couple
that MARY ANN and STAN.

My Sinuses

I am fed up with my
SODDING SINUSES
and
allergies
Nasal sprays,
tablets,
going through
boxes of handkerchiefs.
Coughing, coughing
feeling miserable
Because you're a
SODDING NUISANCE
To me.

Sunshine Poem

How I love the summer
When the sun shines down on me
So much energy
I feel so happy and not so sad
So roll on summer and I will be glad!

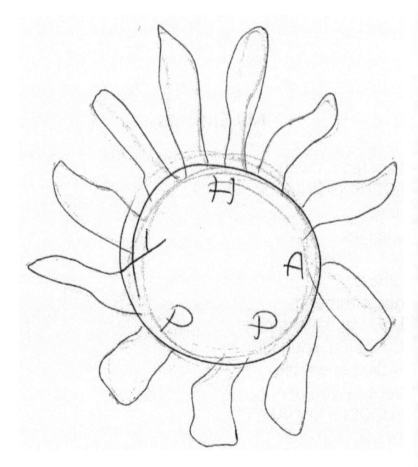

Dwain Bryan

Together! Poet Dwain Bryan writes: "Me I love
Rap music see, and being part of the industry…
Just me and the mike gets the crowd hype
I was influenced by great rappers like Big Smalls
and Busta Rhymes
music is special to be and I love listening to music
I am interested in all kinds of music including Hip
Hop, Soul, R and B and Garage.
For hours on end I can listen to music
I like to get on the Mike and rap as well.
Me, oh yes, me — I'll do anything to get into the
music industry.
Yes me, yes me.
is a part of my soul and mind
it's what wakes me up every morning —
I could copy songs all day long and get a buzz
from every beat!
me and the music are like Brother and Sisters or
Brothers in Arms!"

Rap

I want to do this for the community
Pure unity — love goes out to everybody
We're here to stay so please don't delay
When I sit back and relax
I think of rhyming everyday
I bring my best to the mic and get
The crowd hype we still burning
Like a candle light

Sometimes we ain't always right
But we fight for our rights
Go out to all our mics
In the game and trying to maintain
It's a damn shame ****** like us
Can't be tamed but we remain the best
MCs in the game we're to entertain
And keep the ground moving everyday
We love you you love us
So it goes out to all of you
Who keeps it true and still doing
What you got to do. Sometime it gets
Hard but we keep up our guard
We fabulous we keep on moving
Crush grooving we never losing
We still cruising in those fly-ass jets

I bet your last dollar we are controlling
The set till our last breath
We keep rising climbing to the top
Will never flop hip hop in our blood
So now we're never gonna stop we're gonna keep
Rocking the god damn sport

Until the last blood stain drops

We here to stay swing blows like cactus day
We small hay rest back in the land all day

We're gonna be coming back bigger and better
Don't forget us hash when you see come
So start running cause we remain to stay in the game
And blow your brain.

Titanic Rap 1:
Chained up Sprained up

Chained up, sprained up
Well out of luck
Help me, please, I need room and air to breathe
It was him who stole the thing
Catch him quick
Before he splits

There he goes, watch him go
Look at the thing that he stole

Ring the alarm, but please stay calm
And nobody will be harmed

All I hear is screaming and chaos
Absolutely madness

People rushing around
Sounds like somebody released the hounds.

Titanic Dance Rap

I'm back again in the same old spot
Preparing to rock over the last few days
I've been kind of down, clowning around
The big events coming up soon
And they're waiting for me to arrive
There's going to be a lot of people by my side
This is where I come alive
There's going to be a lot of love and passion
And a lot of action
And we're going to bring you a lot of satisfaction

The crowd's going to be there
I'm going to be there so
Wave your hands in the air like you just don't
care!

Bounce C'mon Bounce C'mon
Bounce C'mon Bounce C'mon

East C'mon West London C'mon
South London C'mon North London C'mon

Blow your horn I said
Blow your horn!

I'm glad you're all here

I'm glad you're all here
To stop and stare
We're here to bring good good vibes in the
atmosphere
When I say 'hey, you all stay
Hey and let the music play'

This is the boat you all been waiting for
I know you're hearing the music and
Making you bounce
I'll sound an ounce to this and now
Smoke in the midst
I hope you're enjoying the show
And listen as we rap
With the flow
We get a classic tonight
So I hope you feel alright
I hope we rock to the sunlight
We'll be la funkular
Ultra funkular jamma ma funkular
It seems like someone ship has done sunkular
So the time has come and I hope you're enjoying
yourself
We're bringing you new stuff in the future
Will be back again to East London Recruiters

Sacrifice

Sacrifice, we all have to sacrifice
Giving up to what we (own)
Creeping, creeping around and trying not to be
noticed—
Searching, trying not to be noticed.
I can see, just about keep moving, trying to keep
moving
I thought I heard something, never mind.
Why? Why? Why?
Me always me. Just not fair
What am I supposed to do now?
No one cares whether I am alone and stranded
Next time I come with a friend to help me throw
back my dark times.
Companion, everyone needs a companion.
Haven't seen you for a while. Where have you
been?
Rest. Which way? West, South, North, East?
Just keep moving.
Boring, so boring.
Something everybody feels like ground hog day.
Music, sweet music.
Music everywhere. Just the sound —
The beat gets me so excited — calms my nerves.
Just a simple song can get the hair on my back

standing up
Take me away, a simple song can just take me
away.
When I'm down and out and feeling low
Music keeps me in control.
What's wrong with you? Why are you acting in
this way?
You'd better stop playing the devil's game.

Kirwin Gibson

Together! Poet Kirwin Gibson is a very talented poet and artist and he attends the Together! Pop-Up Poetry Club, the Together! Art Club and the Art Recovery Group.

Year of change

This is a year of
change in life for me.
This year has been a change
In my life, from the places I go
To the people I meet. And the
gifts I receive, to the gift that
I give, to the food I now eat.

This year so far for me,
Has got me smiling and
Appreciating my life, and
Respecting others' lives too.

I had one cat last year.
Now, I have a dog and a
Kitten, starting with the
Youngest first. The kitten's
name is Misty, the dog's
name is Tara, and she
is the oldest. We are
all capable of mistakes
that's why we have
erasers and pencils. And
the tom cat is called
Gremlin.

And the other
two are both females.
And they are great
company for me, as
I am a bachelor.

Ju Gosling aka ju90

Together! Poet Dr Ju Gosling aka ju90 is an artist, writer and activist and is Artistic Director of Together! 2012 CIC. Ju has been living and working in Canning Town since 1985. She situates her work largely within the theories and traditions of the Disability Arts movement, and has earned an international reputation.
www.ju90.co.uk / @ju90artist

Chains

Some chains I wear gladly
Watching them shine in the light
Some chains I wear sadly
Wet and green with age
Some chains I wear proudly
Holding them high overhead
Some chains I will not wear
Twisting and turning
Pushing and pulling
Shouting and screaming
Until I melt
And slip
Effortlessly
Out.

Same Difference

You said

>"I understand
>"I've known women like you before."

And I heard

>"I know you are a woman
>"A woman like me."

But you meant

>"I know you are different
>"Different like them."

And so I am.

Homecoming

Your presence fills a space I never knew about
You return my love in ways I've never known
The energy we feast on is my life blood
And time has shown that I am not alone.

The world around is hard, but full of beauty
The love I feel protects me as I roam
Though arrows pierce my heart and fire burns me
I'm happy, safe, secure as I come home.

Death of a Poet
(On hearing of the death of David Morris)

He's gone.

The words seem impossible to hear
The thought too hard to bear
The loss too great to realize.
Our poet, our leader, our friend has left without
us.

Left us with art to make
Wars to win
Friends to comfort
But without him.
Without his help, his kindness, his wisdom, his
passion
His love.

Where are the words to explain it?
Where are the thoughts to make sense of it?
Where is our poet, our leader, our friend?

Gone with the sunrise
Gone with the East wind
Gone as the tide turns
Leaving only love, and silence, behind.

Colin Hambrook

Together! Guest Poet Colin Hambrook is author of two illustrated poetry collections: *100 Houses*, DaDaSouth (2011) and *Knitting Time* (Waterloo Press, 2013). He has 20 years experience working at the hub of the Disability Arts Movement as an editor / producer, publishing and showcasing work by disabled artists, fostering networks and enabling debates around the curation and development of disability arts practice.

Growing up with god
(for my daughter)

Recalling your fearlessness
at that age just beyond crawling,
diving down a fifty foot slide
backwards, head first; the buzz
of danger and sheer aliveness.

And now older, revisiting the play park
watching you at home with your world;
and everything looking so much smaller
as if god had shrunk
to the size of an ant;

especially the swinging basket
that once resembled a titan;
the children desperate to get the thing
to roll all the way over its axis,
instilling fear into every parent.

So what is it with the furniture of life?
this patch of grass that was once an acre,
this square mile that held everything,
all expanding and contracting
as if the earth itself had a will of it's own.

Burying beds (for my dad)

Strange it is, watching you shrink
like mud-man left out to dry
under a hot sun.
Preparing for birth,
at the dawn of your closure.
I wonder who will emerge
when the cracks run deep
and the edifice crumbles.

And if I could water
a life at sunset
prolong its fierce aching
who would it serve?
No, at best I hope
to watch you walk
through that door
with a head held high.

After all, I've already seen
you take up a shovel
to cut the rough ground
and make a hole
large enough for a double mattress.
There's nothing new
to your pragmatism
or your fearlessness.

A Map of Life
(for Richard Longstaff)

I never quite believed you'd be leaving us
though I knew the cancer was terminal.
You'd hoped to be able
to put a few thoughts down on the computer
if you found enough strength.

We never met, but talked on the phone
about our families, our fathers and sons
our daughters and wives, cherished;
the line of hopes and fears that moved us
forwards;
the memories that held us to the earth.

And now you've gone, it's like being transported
at speed to a place where life looks map-like
distant, far from the self on a thin chord of poetic
license
defined by the depth of words shared
a love for nature, poetry and truth.

Breathing In
(for Kraean)

You led me to a field of breath
with all its intricate possibilities
for addressing the quandry
of being alive; this forever moment
forever here, forever gone.

I followed your promise of liberation,
down through the rhythm of breath,
absolved by its motion from the nostrils;
into the lungs and further
to the depths of the belly; the centre.

You never learnt to breathe with kindness;
sadly, fell into dangerous cavities
made foolish by a cool intelligence;
and a weapon-like facility for reason.

Years' later you said you had never been loved
in the way that I loved you:
a pasture ripe for forgiveness,
straining for air under an implacable sun.

Ella Higginbottom

Together! Poet Ella Higginbottom is Polish and has lived in Newham for many years. She is a very talented performance poet and artist.

Poem about hmmm

Hmmm….hmmm……hmmm…
I don't count my days,
I don't count my nights
Hmmm…..hmmm…..
It is so slow but it is so fast, hmmm…..
Written by ME……hmmm………!

Damn

This is my leg
       And
This is my arm
Where am I going?
I don't know. Damn!

This is the ink
       And
This is my pen
Can I write a letter to you?
Damn, I can't.

Crocodile shoes,
Caroline chain,
Can you break it?
Damn, I can't.

OK, So You're A Soldier Now

OK, so you're a soldier now,
You have got your green uniform
And you know tomorrow, or today
Or next month you maybe die
They will call you the hero
You will like that or maybe
You don't give a damn
You wouldn't know that birds are
Singing above your grave?
Would you, o' yeah,
Your body started to rot
Would know that o'yeah, now you are dead.
And the men called Muhammed
You know, he was so brave.
But he lost his two legs
But he is a hero now
And the other man
Called John, he's lost his eyesight
and you know what,
 He won't even see his little boy smile.
Be patriotic but smell the flowers
And please, just don't die, not like that one.
Amen.

Even so

Even so
You are sipping your cold brow
Even so
I am scratching myself down below
Even so....
You want to talk...?
OK.
But don't ask me what I feel!!!
What I think!!!
Even so
You will still sip your brow
Even so
I will still scratch myself down
Below
EVEN SO
You don't believe me?
Ask God, he will know.

Yours Sincerely

Crocodile shoes but
Where is the road?
Colombo—is this AMERICA?

Canning Town, Hermit Road—
Good place to live.

Cry for help—
Hey, this is my shoulder...

Jack, dance with me once more
This time for real!

　　　　　　Yours sincerely,
　　　　　　　Ella H.

P.S. Casablanca — I like raw meat

Proverbs

If you have been once in the darkness
You will recognise what light is.
Love is the greatest inspiration.
Only men can change a female to women.
Every drop of water is holy water.

If You have been
once in the Darkness
You will know what
Light is

Belong

There is a place in the bus where I belong;
On the top, on the right, at the front,
Then I am a driver, with Leonard Cohen in my ear.

Wow, fun!!!

This is the place where I belong,
So don't talk too loud
And don't fuckin smell too strong
This is my place...
Am I the driver?

Sarah Hughes

Together! Poet Sarah Hughes is Programme Director for Together! 2012 CIC, having begun as the volunteer project leader for the 2012 Poetry Week. Sarah leads the Pop-Up Poetry Club and says: "Poetry in particular has helped in my artistic development and I hope my work encourages other people to do the same."

Halloween

What's all the fuss about?
Young people scream and shout
There's books and buns and dazzle and fun
But what's it all about?
People dress in black and gore
Their eyes are painted and mouths and more
They look as if they're together in war
They celebrate a dark art but what's in store?
Why do they dance around a lit pumpkin?
Why do they dance without even thinkin?
Is it a celebration or an occasion?
Of good and hope or death and halloweenism?
Why the spider chocolates and scary make up?
Why the dance and going out and scary shake up?
Why the fascination with magic and fake up?
I don't know why, but I don't like it.

Fireworks

Fireworks will light up the sky
They'll zoom, and whizz, and splutter and cry,
They'll pop and bang and whizz and then die
With cries of fascination and laughter and sighs.

Cats and dogs will cower inside
They'll look out at the bright lights but stay firmly inside
Their dark eyes reflect the moonlit night
As sparklers and rockets sprinkle speckles of light.

And out in the atmosphere the planets and the stars
The sun, moon and Saturn, Neptune and Mars
All welcome these visitors that launch into the air
And light up the sky like a meteoric funfair.

So stay out of danger on this brightly lit night
Stay out of trouble and enjoy the beautiful sight
Keep your pets inside and let them sit tight
It's great to see fireworks and it's only one night.

He Will Conquer

Crazy experience
Intense grievance
Unseen shatter
Emotional clatter
Provoked anger
Unspoken hurt
A place of refuge
To re-evaluate and recoil
Recharge and pick up
Take charge and sit up
Don't be broken
Don't be crushed
For God is on your side
And He will conquer.

Unconditional Love

A love that supports
And reports good thoughts
That wraps around
With warmth and sounds of laughter.
A plinth of trust
And loving fuss
That twists away
To sway and pray a warm hope.
A time of grace
Love face to face
A tiny trace of a dance
 to save and sway in comfort.

JAE

Together! Poet JAE is an experienced and gifted poet and lives with her son in Newham.

Glasses

If those glasses are rose tinted
How wonderful that may be
But you may need to take them off
If you need to see the whole me.

As I wear mine, dark and shaded
Like hiding behind a veil
You will need to chip away
As a sculpture with hammer and nail.

You have to lift them
To let the light in
Otherwise we are darkened and cold
Left out there on a limb.

Look at the bigger picture
And how wonderful that can be
Show yourself to the world
And what a colourful brightness you will begin to
see.

I was on my knees
Bruised with the kicking I had given myself.
Dark were shadows of the surrounding corridors
of my mind.

I didn't know how to open the door as I did not
have the keys.
I put them somewhere, possibly hid them.
I clambered manically trying to find them.

Then you knocked. I didn't want to let you in.
I didn't want to answer.
But some inner strength led me over to the door.

I opened it, blinded by the sunlight.
And there stood you.
You told me to take little steps which ached at
first.

Eventually I was able to look for each key to each
door
And I opened the doors to each room
Opened the windows to air my mind, heart and
lungs
 To breathe again

And for that I thank you, Oh God, I thank you.

Leopold Loewer

Together! Poet Leopold Lower is an experienced poet, songwriter and musician. He attends the Together! Pop-Up Poetry Club and Music Club.

Omen of Reckoning

A dream too vivid not to be surreal;
It makes me livid and inclined to reel!

Your affectation of true concern
Sends me graphic (!) to make you learn...

(A) Molecular crash upon your pathway;
My drink is tossed and splashed the whole way!
  Do you get the point and its impression?
Or must I stand attendant to your explanation?
Your attempt at (a) sympathetic expression;
            A Usurper's...condescension.

Rowland Jide Macaulay

Jide Macaulay is the founding Pastor of House Of Rainbow Fellowship. Jide is a British-Nigerian born in London and has been an Anglican Christian minister since 1998. A dynamic and inspirational speaker, author, poet, pastor and preacher, Jide holds a degree in Law, a Masters degree in Theology and a Post-graduate certificate in Pastoral Theology. He has authored two books, *Poetry Inspired* (2001) and *Pocket Devotion for LGBT Christians* (2005).

Jide has won several awards including the 2003 and 2007 Black LGBT Community Award for 'Man of the Year' for his work helping people of faith. Shortlisted for the National Diversity Awards 2014, in the category for Positive Role Model. Winner NAZ MSM Volunteering Award 2014. Jide served from 2007 to 2013 as Executive Board member and Co Chair of Pan Africa International Lesbian and Gay Association. He is currently Co-Chair on the Steering Committee of Global Interfaith Network, Board of Trustee at Kaleidoscope Trust UK, Trained Volunteer Champion at Afruca Children's Charity, and also a Director at Justice for Gay Africans UK.

Poems for My Mother

(1)

Beautiful

Tall African Woman
Playful, jovial in life
Rather than be sad
I will rise and be bad

Beautiful, in heart and soul

My tears flow out of control
No longer sad
I look back at the beauty you gave.

(2)

In memory of a fine lady

Her presence captivates
Her charms no doubt validate
She gave of herself in large measure
That all in her path felt assured

Today, I wept again for you.

I missed all that you always do
Cheeky, jovial and strict
Yet, we never missed a treat
Missing My Mother Again

(3)

Death is impartial but yet selfish.

There is no doubt of the inevitable
The fact that it neither warns nor
When you least expect death strikes
Took my mother away, how frustrating
what fear she experienced in those last moments
Neither do I know when death would visit me
I have no expectations or worry
But what I do know is that I miss her so much
I miss her perhaps now I realise she was the best
Above all the rest
It's too late to appreciate her worth
but rest in her legacy of north
Death is impartial but yet selfish.

Thinking Of Lady Of Shalott

I could not comprehend
The life of Lady Shalott
Whether or not it's a pretty end
It is just too much and quite a lot

In modern time and today
You might be free and gay
Neither judgement nor discrimination to say
Mostly considered the relevance of pay

Thinking of the Lady of Shallot
Brings contention to my soul
But yet there is the Royal court
The distance of thought battered my sole

The precious Lady of Shalott
In her splendid and magnificent beauty
Does give a damn about Lancelot
Never did she abandoned her fundamental duty.

I am a stranger in this land

Leviticus 19:34 "The foreigner residing among you must be treated as your native-born. Love them as yourself, for you were foreigners in Egypt. I am the LORD your God."

I am a stranger in this land
Forgotten and in despair to the band
The band of haters in territorial gang
Safe for the long loving saviours hand
Sadly I would have been trotted to the dang

I am a stranger in this land
Outrageous level of selfish brand
Causes my taste for life to go bland
Event though I thought I could expand
I was denied the opportunity for a farmland

I am a stranger in this land
It simply has become a wishful dreamland
Which has become a mere fantasyland
Fairies who claim the space as their fairyland
Will never stop my wish for a husband

I am a stranger in this land
Though I long for my motherland

In the same place I am casted in to dry land
Being queer is a lifetime demand
My loyalty constantly denied and considered
disband.

Prayer:

God of consolation,
look on us, pilgrims in a strange land;
preserve us from slander and deceit,
show us the truth
and give to our souls the peace of Christ.

Angus McKenzie-Davie

Together! Poet Angus McKenzine-Davie originally trained as an actor in the early 80s. In 1995 he became disabled, contracting ataxia, a neurological disease, and spent a year in hospital rehabilitating. After this he became an advocate for disabled rights, promoting the rights of disabled people and trying to mitigate the attacks being made on the people most at risk in our society.

War & Disability:
War transforms attitudes to disability

Before the First World War, disabled people were isolated and seen as the 'deserving poor'.
Not only have this century's wars created a large number of disabled people, but a shortage of workers in the Second World War prompted many companies to hire staff with disabilities.

The Second World War gave impetus to the feminist movement; but it also played a major part in transforming people's views of disability. During the Second World War, many disabled people who were not deemed fit for work were suddenly valued as workers because of acute shortages in the labour force.

The disabled veteran is not seen in popular culture as a limited person, as most other people with disabilities are. He/she were "whole" before their injury, and were cut down in the prime of youth while fighting for their country, and making the world safe.

Headstrong Big War

Still caught in the grip of this madness.
Where the walls move in, and the floor turns into
a sea.
And you could just fall in and drown.

And all you can think of is getting back to the
jungle.
Walking through the trees.
Waiting for some man with a knife to rush out.
Wanting to look at you and kill.

Just stuck in a little room,
Partitioned in a hut made out of wood.
That burns so easily,
When someone drops napalm on your head.

Still walking through the jungle.
You've been home three times.
But that doesn't work now.
Because you just want to get back here,
Waiting for someone to rush out,
So you can kill.

Headstrong Big War, Headstrong Big War.
Headstrong Big War, Headstrong Big War.

The volume of serious injuries during war leads to significant improvements in acute care and gives doctors and nurses practical skills in treating them. After war, rehabilitative medicine works with disabled soldiers and veterans.

Built Like A Chair

Smell of oil, slippery and black.
Jack her up, cauterise the wound.
I'm not disabled, because of her.
My own vampire.
Teeth so sharp, makes my reach so long.

Smooth curves, sleek and shiny.
The womb I ride inside.
Wheels make tracks inside my mind,
Broken and muddy, but sparkling in the darkness.
Run my hand carefully over explosive skin.
Life incarnate.

Smell of gears, it's the smell of sex.
Life created by death, born of war.
Explosive love, orgasmic destruction.
Fear her loss, need her.

Dominated, emasculated.
Strike because of fear.
Money talks, money kills.
But baby will help destroy them all.
Smack, baby, smack.
Help annihilate the creator's hand.

Over the years, 'rehabilitation' has come to mean many things, from relearning the daily tasks of personal care, (the Medical Model of disability) to rethinking the physical environment in which people with disabilities live. (the beginnings of the Social Model of Disability) We are still fighting this battle, it is ironic that advances in disabled rights can stem from such destruction.

Borneo

Malay peninsula
Brother died in Malay
I fucking hate Americans, they don't know how to
say hello, just bang. That's not the way to say
hello
Traumatised
Brown, Blair and the other one
That bastard
Blair's unhappy
Truth is like a knife
It cuts away lies
Can't do that from records.

Navy man

I was a young man
Rough Brigade
Sukarno
Something special
You don't know what you've found
I am a clean man, but what I've done
It was bad
So now you know about me, and you are correct
And now you can learn more.

Jon T. Light

American, CIA
I come from a terrible family
Terrible
Long ago was a….whoo!
It's true long time ago
Dreadful, unbelievable, horrible
Old time
They were horrible people
When they killed that king, they murdered the
king, I know what they did
It had to be done
I'm nicer, im not that way
Tell me the truth
I'm a nice little fellah
I'm better than them
But what could I do against that?
We're meant to be nice to each other
What's wrong with being nice?
I've been in battle
You can tell by this tin leg
Why cant we be nice to each other?
We can make life unbelievably nice.

All those friends, Bluebelle.
Harlem princess, and black
Wish she were here
Wish they were all back
Not buried in the war, long dead
Can you believe how hard they can bring a hand
down?
Wanna do something useful, something good
Put it all in
Good for humankind
And the truth? How bad am I?
I'm a nice man.

People who suffered shell shock in the First World War were classed as mentally ill. If they were badly affected, they were sent to a mental home. In World War Two and thereafter, diagnosis of 'shell shock' was replaced by that of combat stress reaction, a similar but not identical response to the trauma of warfare.

More recently we had the Persian Gulf Wars, which left thousands of vets with a variety of ill-nesses commonly known as Gulf War Syndrome or Post Traumatic Stress Disorder. Approximately 250,000 of the 697,000 U.S. veterans who served in the 1991 Gulf War are affected by Gulf War Syndrome. The US department of Veterans Affairs acknowledges that Gulf War veterans suffer from chronic and ill-defined symptoms, including fatigue and neurocognitive and musculoskeletal problems. The Pentagon admits that 100,000 US troops were exposed to low levels of nerve gas.

Exposure to Agent Orange during the Vietnam war is even now affecting veterans 40 years later with increased risk of developing diabetes, Alzheimers disease and a range of other conditions.

Rubble

A dark night over London
The fires have all burned down
The blitz is over for a while
And the fabric of the underworld has been torn
away
Flickering shadows, yellow and black, and red
blood
A passage through the impassable has been
created
This passage is evil and smooth, a fire over the
Styx
A tunnel to Hades, and the land of shades
Yellow and black, a fire born in hell

Shadows walk among the piles of newly created
rubble
Worshippers of a new fast forward frontier
Quickly created instant entropy
That comes from the belly of an aeroplane
Still burning pyres and twisted blocks of shattered
masonry
Chaotic terrain, assimilating everything

A shadow in the flickering firelight
As the dust settles, the rubble moves, parts

And a black shape slides upward into the night
that is no longer dark
Parting the shattered bricks and woodwork with
long sinuous fingers
A crushed leg is no impediment
It forces its way into this new uncompleted world
And sniffs the sulphurous air.

While celebrating advances made in the disability movement, we should never forget that in the armed conflicts of recent years, children have been not only unintended victims but also deliberate targets of violence. Millions of children have been killed, disabled, orphaned, sexually exploited and abused, abducted and recruited as soldiers, uprooted from their homes, separated from their families, and faced with heightened risk of disease and malnutrition.

Shall I?

Shall I compare thee to a half-track tank
I can't pierce your body armour
But if you set your sights on me
I'd be helpless in your radar

I love your wheels, so please don't kill me
I could be your zimmer yet
Hold you up all through this conflict
You're a sniper, I'm the target

John O'Donoghue

Together! Guest Poet John O'Donoghue is the author of *Brunch Poems* and *Fools & Mad* (Waterloo Press, 2009 and 2014), and *Sectioned: A Life Interrupted* (John Murray, 2009), which was awarded Mind Book of the Year 2010. He teaches Creative Writing at the University of Westminster and lives in Brighton.

Poet For Our Time
after Carol Ann Duffy

After eighteen years of total misrule –
And do not think we'll ever forget her –
We turned to spin to make us look cool,
Singing THINGS CAN ONLY GET BETTER.

And on our way to everyone winning –
Everyone that is who made a donation –
We were all so brilliantly spinning:
EDUCATION, EDUCATION, EDUCATION.

For we needed to move in a new direction,
And clearly this was to be our time,
For we alone could make the connection:
TOUGH ON CRIME, TOUGH ON THE CAUSES OF
CRIME.

And to show that we still had the common touch
A fondness for rock stars, football, and bitter –
We drove round in jags and threw a mean punch
And shouted: I'M A FIGHTER, NOT A QUITTER!

So take heart from our spinning, and don't
despair,
Even if you don't share all of our views:

Though questions are asked and journalists blare
THIS IS A GOOD DAY TO BURY BAD NEWS.

For when all is said at the end of the day
We gave you a Britain that is fair and just,
A Britain that's better in every way,
Our proudest boast: AN END TO BOOM AND
BUST!

The Cost Of Sanity
after Dietrich Bonhoeffer

I spoke to the voices – they confused me.
I spoke to the doctor – he diagnosed me.
I spoke to the psychiatrist – she sectioned me.
I spoke to the nurse – he medicated me.
I spoke to the social worker – she assessed me.
I spoke to the housing officer – he resettled me.
I spoke to the benefits adviser – she referred me.
I spoke to the key worker – he reviewed me.
I spoke to the probation officer – she paroled me.
I spoke to the policeman – he arrested me.
I spoke to the magistrate – she sentenced me.
I spoke to the prison officer – he confined me.
I spoke to the walls – they ignored me.
I spoke to the voices – for now there was no one
else…

Do Not Go Gentle

Do not go gentle into this good fight,
This age should burn and rave at banker's pay;
Rage, rage against the lying of the Right.

Though wise men say we can't avoid our plight
Why should we listen to a word they say?
Do not go gentle into this good fight.

Good men, from days gone by, crying how bright
Their children might have danced in a green bay,
Raged, raged against the lying of the Right.

Strong men who picketed Wapping day and night
And fought with Rupert Murdoch all the way,
Did not go gentle into this good fight.

Brave men, Up North, who saw with blinding sight
The mines closed down and their shovels thrown
away,
Raged, raged against the lying of the Right.

And you, my comrades, here with me tonight,
Know that the struggle will not go away.
Do not go gentle into this good fight:
Rage, rage against the lying of the Right.

From An Asylum Diary

The day staff arrive about six-thirty,
Wake us at seven. I still feel dirty,
Though the sheets are clean, though I bathed last
night,
Dregs of dreams still draining from my pop-eyed
Brain, body sore as if from frantic fight.
Another day starts, the ward stirs, we're plied
With candy-coloured drugs to stop us from
Seeing life as candy-coloured. We come
Down the stairs after breakfast hungover
From tedium, the strain of this mad life.
The Black girl wishes it was all over,
Will try to slash her wrists with a sneaked knife.
The ward is quiet. Undercurrents are rife.

Occupational therapy starts at
Nine. I'm on the gardens, pass a black cat
On my way to the hut. My wellies clump
And shudder as I stride along. The rest
Are already sat drinking tea, a slump
Of a paddy and a cockney possessed
By some manic devil. Gaunt as a pressed
Leaf he cannot keep still. Not at his best
Today, off form, cagey, Pat's growling
(Side effects) and I'm an interloper

Listening to his tales, how he built, scowling
Now, half the fuckin' country, a pauper
Here, in for life, what they call a 'no-hoper'.

The green fields always bring release. We keep
Them short as lawns, potter about half asleep,
Filching litter into floppy black plastic
Bags, raking leaves, trimming the edges on
The long, stone-lipped swathe of grass (fantastic
Panorama from up here) which sweeps sun-
Lit up to the main entrance, purposeful,
Pretending to control, to be useful.
The boss, a Pole, has told us of his wife, who
Died last spring. Already grief has started
To diminish and disfigure him, to
Remind us all that the broken-hearted
Are like us, live too close to be parted.

I come back from the morning's chores, the ward
Collecting in a queue, straggly and bored,
Outside the dining room upstairs, other
Patients from the rest of this small unit
Talking, smoking, shuffling. A young mother
Is wailing for her children, staff punitively restrain
her, break her will. We're here
For cracking and have less than her to fear,
But no one helps her – she's alone. We know

Well the bright array of needles in their
Cabinets, have seen opposition go
To pieces with one quick jab. There's an air
In here of indolence everywhere.

I've been to see a half-way house, expect
To be discharged soon. Today two guys wrecked
The office, went beserk and put the wired
Window in. I'm waiting for the finance
To come through, am nervous and overtired,
Hoping I won't be knocked back. Went to the
dance
Last night, worked off that damned largactyl, the
sweat
Running like drizzle down my forehead, set
Off for chores again this morning feeling
Fucked. All the nurses have gone back to school
Now, except the old hands who are dealing
Out the small pills and exercising rule.
At night I dream I'm drowning in a pool.

Sarifa Patel

Together! Poet Sarifa Patel writes: "I am an Asian disabled women who is an activist around empowering Asian and BME disabled women whose voices are not being heard, epecially when they are allies and carers to their loved ones who may also have complex health needs.

Right from the start

You were so beautiful! How could we not love
you?
This system wanted to destroy you
Right from the start.
Looking at your handsome smile
The special bond we develop, the constant
negativity around your birth
They wanted our relationship destroyed.
My children, how much I fought
the constant pressure they endured on me to
have an abortion as you may cost too much.
Right from the start
we had to fight united.
Luckily my own experience around my impairment
taught me a valuable lesson.
Don't trust them, it's your body. You are the
expert patient.
Believe in your own inner strength
Right from the start.
They're little people would bring some amazing
resilience and strength
If they could survive against the odds.
Why can't you leave it in God's hand
Right from the start.
No more abortion.

No more pressure for us mothers.
We are vulnerable at that time.
We need you to support us.
We need you to say it's going to be fine
Not adding additional pressure
around our future.
Our children bring gifts, you know.
Let our children be.
Right from the start.
Maybe they have differences.
So what, they are still our flesh and blood.
They deserve to be wanted, like any other child in
the world.
They need to be protected
from a society that's so cruel,
which wants to take away their Human Rights to
life.
Let our children be.

Sterre Ploeger

Together! Poet Sterre Ploeger is an actor, poet and musician.

A Poem about People

People   make   me   happy

Meeting   people

Saying Hi

People   make   me   happy

Going out

With my   friends

People   make   me   happy

Talk to   me

Using signs

because people make   me   happy!

Glory Sengo

Together! Poet Glory Sengo writes: "I am 22 years old and I come to the Together! Art and Poetry groups. I am very inspired by Congolese musicians, especially Joly Mubiala, Koffi Olomide, Modogo Ferre and Papa Wemba.

Fireworks!

Being more funny since I was at home cleaning up the house in the morning and I also turned on the stereo and started playing music!

But I went on a laptop to search for my friend on Facebook.

Then I was having a headache and it was Sarah Omoraka and she told me if it is OK that what have you been doing ?

"Cleaning up the house and mopping up the floor."

"Oh that's nice."

"Thank you. You're in my room."

"Yes, yes."

"Come on then. Here we are. I need to do something at the moment. How's your mum?"

"OK."

"Your sister and your brother?"

"He's good. I love you, Glory."

"I love you too, Sarah."

"You promised to kiss me."

"Yes, Sarah. What else have you been up to?"

"Searching for my friend John Lamming ."

"Oh, that's great. That's nice. Black shorts. Thank you, Glory."

"You're welcome. Glory, what a nice white vest.

Glo, thank you. I really love your white vest sell."
"Thank you, sell."

The Snake Poem

When I first travelled the snake bar
and I was walking down to the **jungle**
to see a **snake** around the world
when it was in a day
and I was scared of a **wooden bird**.
They were doing their own business
and it flew over me and jumped
and everybody wondered 'What was that?'
But everyone knew that it was a **ghost**.

And my friends went to me 'Was that you?'
'Yes, it was me' Because I was brave enough
not to be scared of a **snake**
and I was in bed in a **jungle**
still dreaming about a place in *Ireland*.

Poem about Music

When I was in Canning Town watching TV
  then it was
    Matou Samuel
      but after that it was
      Koffi Olomide
        and he was singin
        Ngola na nzambe
          from KCC and then
          Naomie
          from
          'Wake up in Papa Wemba'
        and I went in my mum's room to see dad
      while his eyes were closed and he was
    sleeping and I went to sleep too.
  And before that **Matou Samuel**
  was singing in English.
  I must find out about it and
Naomie
too.

The Pigeons

When I was outside walking then the ***wooden bird*** flew over and I was like **"Arrh!"** and the **pigeon** was on me and started biting me and it didn't do nothing.

Then I was bloody going to my **girlfriend**'s house in Custom House to have a long chat with ***Bianca Butcher*** and we was having a drink with each other. We was **acting normal**. We went to the living room to watch TV which is **rubbish**. Finders keepers!

And we were **acting crazy** and we were looking at each other and started **kissing each other** again and started playing and I've grabbed her so that I'll be pretending that I was carrying her **like she was a baby** and I've **kissed her** on the lips because we were eating **sausage** and **chips** and **beans**.

John Simmonds

Together! Poet John Simmonds writes: "I like writing poetry as I hope to inspire people into being creative and positive in life. I believe that God is love and that we have an eternal soul. I do not think there is such a thing as normal. Thank God."

Nothing Ever Dies

You are deep in my heart
We are never far apart
I have a distant goal
You have the key to my heart
I have spiritual needs
They are sown like seeds
Among the reeds
Give me time to forget it ain't no joke
I was nearly broke.
I have like you an eternal soul
I am a one off
Sometimes you may think I am a disgrace
I am brave and no one's slave
A day with the Lord is like one thousand years
Sometimes I shed tears
I am happy when you are near
I must conquer all my fears
So shed no tears
Jesus is near.

Eternal Life

Have I lived before? Will I live again? All have asked these questions.
Who am I? Am I the name I was christened with? Am I the present body I have?
The challenges I have had. People I have met.
How do I know what to believe? Is self belief everything? We rightly or wrongly believe in God.
According to your belief , be it done unto you.
I need the right company. If the world ends, what will happen to consciousness?
If the universe is mathematical, then so am I. My watch tells me the time.
Am I consciousness only?

Allan Sutherland

Together! Guest Poet Allan Sutherland is an award-winning writer and passionate poet and a long-time member of the Disability Arts movement.

Slain with the Spirit

The healer cures the little child:
He tells her, "Jesus says get up and walk".
The child gets up. She walks.
The crowd goes wild.

The choir sings, "Oh, Praise the Lord!"
The organs blare. Collecting tins
Go round. The healer says,
"This child is cured."

The child says, "I use a chair
But I can walk. I always could.
I know my legs are weak,
But they're still there."

The crowd can't hear above the din.
The healer hears, but doesn't care;
He knows it's not the child
Who puts the money in the tin.

The Big C

(For Angela, who was told not to write from experience)

'C is for chickweed and Chile and chess
Computers and corgis and cowboys and cress
Clamber and cuddle and canter and caper
Crystals and constables, cod and crepe paper

'C is for custard, a considerable portion
And coming to class with commendable caution
Cartesian co-ordinates, Christian charity
Chimneys and cellars and cabbage and clarity

'So why can't you write about something that's nice?
Cherries or chocolate or coconut ice
Consomme or chump chops, cream crackers and cheese
We don't mind if you write about subjects like these.

'We'd just like you to keep everything in proportion
Caravans, crosswords, connubial caution,
Carpets and catfood and cavalry twill -

These are the things that will give us a thrill.

'Frankly, what you want to say is outrageous.
We don't think about illness — It might be
contagious.
Poetry's comfortable, timid and bland
We write with our heads firmly stuck in the sand.'

'I'm beginning to see what you mean by this
chant
C is for censorship, C is for cant.
I find your suggestions less than inviting
I want to write about something exciting.

'Ceilidh and carnival, cha-cha and conga
Cocaine and Cointreau and coral from Tonga
Canoes full of cannabis, commedia dell'arte.
Come out of the closet and come to the party.

'Cunnilingus for Christmas, concertina and candle
C for the coast of Coromandel
Comedy, cider and Charlie the cat.
And C is for cancer — What's wrong with that?'

Song for a Recalcitrant Bus Driver

She's got places to go, she's got things to do
(The train leaves for Brighton at quarter past two)
Not wait on the pavement admiring the view.
That's why the lady needs the ramp.

She's doing the things she chooses to do.
She's going to the Tate and the Whitechapel too.
She doesn't take any nonsense from you.
That's why the lady needs the ramp.

She's taken trouble dressing up fine,
She's planning to taste the fruits of the vine
And conversation more exciting than mine.
That's why the lady needs the ramp.

We fought for these spaces in midsummer heat,
Blocked all the traffic on New Oxford Street.
There weren't any pushchairs patrolling that beat.
That's why the lady needs the ramp.

She's socialising, out and about.
She's getting on here, you be in no doubt.
So tell all those pushchairs they'd better move out
Because the lady needs the ramp!

Social Workers

I hate the social workers, I tell you,
because they have done wrong to me.

They have done wrong to me
and they know they shouldn't have
done this to me.

I've got every right to see my kids,
to see how they are and, you know,
I just don't like charity workers.

Anyone talks about charity workers to me,
I don't want to know.

They've done a bad job, really,
towards a mother like me,
done a bad job, really bad job.

They should have come down to my house
and talked to me
and tell me how my son is and,
but no I don't want to be nearby none of them.

So I don't want nothing to do
with social workers no more,

Nothing,
they're crap as far as I'm concerned, you know.

But, you know
every social worker who's listening to this,
everybody who knows about this
should know about it .

I should let everybody know about this,
because it's so hurtful,
it's all hurtful, you know.

They shouldn't have done it in the first place,
really, you know, because that is denigration
to a mother like me, with learning difficulties.

And I just feel right now,
some of it is saying to me,
half of me is saying, Jennifer
you should have your son back with you.

But it's not that easy
to have your son back with you,
it's not that easy.

(Transcription poem from the words of Jennifer
Taylor.)

Bite the Hand That Feeds You

Frank is a nice boy
He never makes a fuss
Frank spends all his time at home
He can't get on the bus

    Bite the hand that feeds you
    Make the bugger bleed
    Then maybe they'll notice you
    And ask you what you need

Terry can't stand cripples
They fill him full of fear
But raising money on their behalf
Is good for his career

    Bite the hand that feeds you
    Make the bugger bleed
    He doesn't care a toss for you
    He does it out of greed

If tugging at your forelock
Is making no impression
Don't think that Lady Bountiful
Will counter your oppression

Bite the hand that feeds you
Make the bugger bleed
You don't get rights without a fight
So fight for what you need

Lajeaune Wright

Together! Poet Lajeaune Wright writes: "I am 25 years old. I am a special girl and I've loved every moment of my life, the ups and downs. I like my physio in the morning, and I love my shower. I like music and I like to go out. I prefer to spend time out from my 'car'. I'm not always in a good mood, but I'm sure this is the same for everyone. I am a special girl with a very special mum."

Poems with Victorita

What I would like to do today?
Is just to go away
To have a lovely funny day
With my friends in Calais.

Bowling

It's raining, it's cold and dark
I can't go today in the park.
But it's no problem because I think
To go in Ilford to play bowling.

Song

The yapa yapa yeppa
I need a piece of paper
The tapa tapa ten
And I would like a pen
To write this short poem.

S'il te plaît

Ahh! It's time for my rest.
But I would like to go in the sensory room,
Come and help me to leave this chair
Do some physio, please, and tidy up my hair
Everyone can listen to my favourite song.
Fluffy, my neighbour's cat, looks big.
Grass in my garden needs to be cut
Hey, redoing my hair, please do a plait.
I want to look pretty today, s'il te plaît
Jasmine, my friend, will be visiting me.

Westfield (with Yvonne)

Spent the whole day out.
Going up and down and around and about
East, west, north and south
Mostly West, in fact.
Westfield shopping centre.
Where you need lots of money to enter
For all the shops on offer
With lots of stuff they proffer
Went to the Olympic Park for fresh air
Cos of course 't'was quite near
Enjoyed the lovely sunshine
Then we went to dine.
Went shopping in Primark
Bought a tracksuit — 't'was quite dark.
Laughed, coughed and chatted my way home.
Tomorrow another day to roam.

Wendy Young

Together! Guest Poet Wendy Young is a regular Performance Poet at Survivors' Poetry and other London poetry events and writes "Poetry with oomph". She recently performed at Outside In, Chichester. She writes reviews and blogs for DAO. Wendy has also published in *South Bank Poetry*, *Poetry Express*, *Anomalie Magazine* and *Poetry Rivals*.

I Don't Feel Like Trippin' Tonight

Imagine going down the kebab shop and letting it
all out
When the man say's 'yes darling what would you
like?'

I'll have a 'vent my spleen'
Dish of the day
That's number 666
From the Angry Takeaway
Add a d to anger
You've got danger
Take the c from charmed and
You've got harmed
(Oops I did it again
Got lost in my harm)
Meant to say
Take the ch from charmed
And I am armed
So that's one armed and
Extremely dangerous please!

I'm not taking a drug with 'trip' in it
Whether it's tripping light fantastic
Or tripping me up
I'd rather have an Angry Takeaway

Hope is my drug
Euphoria for me is blasting past bad memories
Here in the moment I am free
Free at last! God almighty free at last!

Sea'scape Shuttle

I wish I'd been born at the bottom of the sea
Nobody there to bother me
The only rattling in my ears
Would be the conch and the Cuttle's encounter
What bliss to swim with angel fish
And kiss piranhas
On a subliminal bite to ecstasy

Past is a Prison

The past is a prison
Now I'm breaking free
Using bad memories positively
Letting it flow
Letting it go
Happy to be me

I won't be selfish
Let's all do it
Find some therapy
Be your inner poet:

Poetry, how do I love thee?
Let me rhyme the ways
Deal with hesitation
Do a recitation
For life's reclamation
Positive for the nation
Read, write, hear, think poetry!

Sleep Bomb

Sleep
Deep
Blue
Water
Ebbing
Flowing
Going
Coming
Back
To front
Door
Slamming
Damning
Sleep
Needed
Impeded
Imps
And shepherds
Run away
Runaways
Joan Jett
Black
Out of it out of it out it…you're in a rut

You won't

Let me sleep
Till I write
What I think
No rest
For distressed
Poetique
Head hold
I'll burst
Till I get
Get you out
T-mobile
Envelope
Next to my bed
Bull's notrils
Breath out with relief
Bulls breath nostrils thyroid thumping words corti-
sone crush strangling me till I strike with my Bic
Time I used
Up all the ink
You were sick
Emetic
Cleared the crap
Emit Emit!
Inner shit
Cathartic
Psychosis
Psycho Sis

Get her out
Better this
Than reminisce
Now is bliss
Now is bliss
See me tick
See me tick
Tick tock
Tock tick
See me rock
Rrrrock rrrock
Time bomb
Big bang
You rang
My bell
My bell
Goes ring
Ring wrong
big bang
BANG BONG